laughter includes the word

revealed, a life of poetry

by doug snelson ⟵

Hi its my Neighbors brother

edited by matthew wilkes

"The poems of Doug Snelson came as a surprise. I embraced their originality from the moment I began reading them, one by one. I was immediately taken by Snelson's individualistic view of things and his ability to make our old words work again, even to sing. His distinctive vision, with its emphasis on the ordinary life around us, is well worth the reading. This poet accomplishes what every poet should aspire toward—he instructs on how to see and hear with aplomb."

—Neeli Cherkovski

*Well-known poet and memoirist **Neeli Cherkovski** is the author or editor of more than 20 books of poetry and was awarded the 2017 Jack Mueller Poetry Prize by Lithic Press for a lifetime of poetry devotion and excellence. He is the biographer and friend of Charles Bukowski and Lawrence Ferlinghetti. Neeli is also the author of "Whitman's Wild Children," a collection of essays about twelve poets he has known, including Charles Bukowski, Gregory Corso, Lawrence Ferlinghetti, Allen Ginsberg, Bob Kaufman, and Michael McClure.*

Acknowledgements

Thanks to Matthew Wilkes for his friendship, insight, and eagle eye in editing this body of work and to Eric Siry, for his creativity and attention to detail with the design layout.

Published by Petalous Publishing, LLC
PO Box 285, Farmingdale, NJ 07727

Library of Congress Control Number: 2018942258
ISBN: 978-0-9777811-3-3

Printed in the United States of America

First Edition

Books by Doug Snelson are available at bulk discounts for schools. The author is also available for customized reading programs.

For more information, please email via contact at dougsnelson.com

For Diane, Ryan, and Renée

Introduction

I thought everyone wrote poetry—my friends, my family, my classmates, new people I met, people I never knew. I always thought each of them, like me, had a tattered black gym bag that was the receptacle of innermost thoughts written on notepads, envelopes, loose-leaf binder paper, torn spiral notebook pages, napkins and random scraps of paper.

At some point I learned most people don't write down their experiences as they happen and certainly not in a poetic sense. Perhaps I was going through a phase in my late teens and twenties yet I continued to add to my gym bag—one poem at a time until now—and I continue on.

Through the years I would pull out my Olivetti typewriter and compile my poems in some order. Computers had me organizing them again in the 80's, and again, and again.

These poems, these expressions of my heart, mind, and soul, became my best friends. Each poem reflects a moment in time for me and was written in real time over 50 years.

Included in this collection are copies of original handwritten drafts as well as original typewritten drafts from my Olivetti typewriter. Each poem is accompanied by a brief commentary about the circumstances of its composition and the year it was written.

My hope is for you to find and enjoy a friendship with one of my poems—perhaps a phrase or a line or a feeling. My hope is you will create your own expression via the world of words. My hope is we all will learn the exact meaning of words so we can understand each other better.

—DS

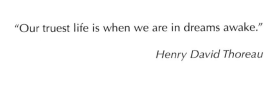

"Our truest life is when we are in dreams awake."

Henry David Thoreau

Table of Contents

(sitting close   sign of the cross
watching the one o'clock movie -)

charlotte elliott and fredric
march climbed cecille b. deville's
dog steps into the roman arena -
close
the lions ate them
charles laughton ceasered his
smile ~~laughed~~ with the christian blood.

the sign of the cross
seemed far illogical to romans
and it seems so illogical to
me at times
but i ~~cried~~ laughed ~~while~~ i cried
~~the moment your eyes~~ made me cry
~~when he slept~~ when he slept of Aurore de Borzee,
~~then~~ he died in the play.

(and then the show ran -
the blessed company went too weary
~~when~~ or they will shut the gleaming.

sign of the cross

sitting alone
watching the one o'clock movie
claudette colbert and fredric march
climbed cecil b. demille's
long steps into the roman arena

alone

the lions ate them

charles laughton ceasared his
smile with the christian blood

the sign of the cross

seemed so illogical to me
at times

(and then the telephone rang—
the telephone company wants their money
or they will turn the service off)

The Sign of the Cross *was a black and white film from 1932. I watched a*
rerun on our black and white TV. The movie ended and the phone rang.
I was told my parents were behind in paying the telephone bill and the
service would soon be turned off. I wrote this on a calendar pad. (1966)

the great american hamburger
is sandwiched between
buns and hamburger's
luncheonette
the pet of hot afternoons
and rich grilled aves,
the child of oh tasty
candy bars, and coke,
(simply) said dream..
~~[crossed out line]~~
there he stood naked in his
back yard munching on a
grilled cheese sandwich and
gulping down a vanilla
shake-)
and the great american hotdog
is yankee leo's friend
made of driedbones and anfined bay
chosen.
he slops it down with relish
and kraut
a bath ... his saye untinty
of ketchup and a malted-elred milk
(by you the greate) the thing
i petto so set my onli that the thing
on that

the great american hamburger

the great american hamburger
is sandwiched between sears and bamberger's luncheonette—
the pet of hot afternoons and rich grilled cars, the child of oh
henry! candy bars and coke

"simplify" said thoreau
as he stood naked in his backyard
munching on a grilled cheese sandwich
and pumping down a vanilla shake

and the great american hot dog
is man's best friend made of
dried bones and orphaned hog chops

he slops it down with relish and kraut
he's never without a bottle of red ketchup
and a multi-colored smile

"hey, you gotta quarta?
i gotta go get my orda"

"here you are, mr. thoreau,
the great american hamburger!"

"that's strange,
no change
that's strange,
no change"

no change
no change
no change

A need to express two opposing thoughts. (1967)

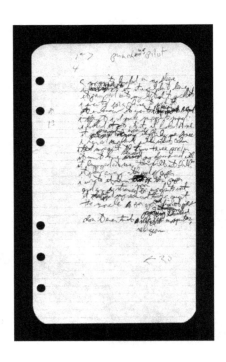

a mosquito landed on my sleeve

a mosquito landed on my sleeve,
i frowned at it, it wouldn't leave

it jumped onto my left shirt pocket
i waited for a chance to sock it

i knew it wanted precious blood,
i thought i'd make mosquito mud

i looked at it,
it looked at me,
it preyed upon my left leg knee

i raised my hand with silent calm,
i told mosquito the two-three psalm

it must have sensed my downward will,
it buzzed at me, "thou shalt not kill"

it flew away, the end of caper
i wrote it down upon this paper

and as i strained for words to sort,
it bit my neck and took a quart

the moral for you blessed discreet joes,
don't ever trust religious mosquitoes

This actually happened to me, so I wrote it down. (1967)

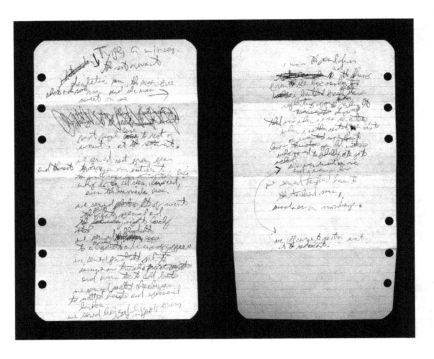

pearl diver

diabetic sam, the sugar-free coke,
short-order cook man,
said she was sweet on me

most people came to rest
to want at the restaurant

we served rest from daily fear
the rest of our kitchen was simple life to the waitress's ear
they all seemed more divorced from their lives
than from their husbands

we served lots of want (the blue plate special)
and the single counter stool

we served early morning bloodshot eggs to a crushed cigarette
and a cup of coffee to an empty mind

we served frustrated pie crusts to innumerable trucks
and warm tea to cold busts

we served cheeseburgers to melted hearts
and ephemeral larks
we served lies and lies of fries each friday night
to the basic wants of everyman

i was the pearl diver
i stole shrimp from icebox number two
I breathed fresh soup-stained stars reflecting from the parking lot disposal

i was seventeen

i neither rested a minute
nor wanted more than to know
the nineteen-year-old waitress
who moved to philly to go to school

she was sweet on me and I thought i was in love

most people came to rest to want at the restaurant

we served taylored ham to the tailored man,
and with sundaes on mondays

*During my summer job for college at the King & Queen Restaurant and Diner
in Wayne, NJ. A "pearl diver" is one who washes pots and pans. (1968)*

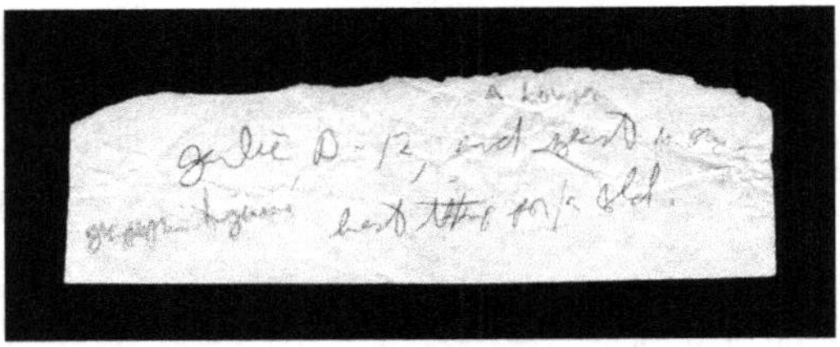

a howism

garlic

B-12

and yeast in

grapefruit juice

best thing for a cold

*My father taught me to squeeze the glove
when catching a baseball, to use the backboard
when shooting a basketball from six feet or
closer, and to count the boards to the left of
the black diamond each time before rolling
a bowling ball down the lane. He was an
avid listener of Dr. Carlton Fredericks, a radio
commentator and writer on nutrition and health.
Dad took all of the good doctor's advice and
decided he knew the cure for a cold. (1968)*

i gained a friend
   (which was nice)

we talked until ...
... and each time knew
that a friend ... only once
is won twice

i gained a friend

   (which is ...)
we ... that ...
of ... stated ... will not ...
... how long ...
not true

i gained a friend
   (which is ...)
... both ... of ...
and ... to think ... i
could tell
... the ... of life
can be ...

i gained a friend
   (which is ...)
we talked until ...
that ... give ... tell
... and ...
... not ...
... until end

i gained a friend

   (which was nice)
we talked until two
and ... 10-6-30
that a friend only
once won ...

10

i agained a friend

i agained a friend
(which is nice)

we talked until two
and each one of us knew
a friend is only once
never twice

i agained a friend
(which is rare)

we rehashed those old times
of some wild oats crimes
and how easy it is
not to care

i agained a friend
(which is bad)

we both spoke of our hell
and to him i could tell
the heaven of life
can be sad

i agained a friend
(which is grand)

we thanked friend in the sky
we're friends 'til we die
and we thanked one sweet word—
understand

i agained a friend
(which is nice)

we talked until two
and each one of us knew
a friend's only once
never twice

For my best childhood friend, Mark, in the summer
between college years after a visit. (1969)

Dear Mom,

                    TO ME MUDDA.

Who gives me naigs and 'acon with
    sliced hot dogs and salami......

                            MOMMY!

Who spreads Skippy on me sandwich
    and cuts dem wit da cutter......

                            PEANUT MUTTER!

Who takes me on da swimmin' trips
    from Jersey ta Alabammy.........

                            MAMMY!

Who gave me a sister when I had a
    Daddy and two brothers..........

                            MOTHER!

Who puts the bandages on my hurts
    when I sprains my ankle like a dummy...

                            MUMMY!

Who cleans da doit from my doity shoit
    when I falls into da gudder......

                            MUDDER!

Who do I love da most in da roughsies
    and da calmsies................

                            MOMSIES!

                    Love,   Douglas Snelson
                              Doug
                              Syracuse University
                              May 8, 1969
                              8:01 P.M.

to me mudda (may 8, 8:01 pm)

who give me "naigs an' 'acon" with sliced hot dogs and salami.....
mommy!

who spreads skippy on me sandwich and cuts dem wit da cutter.....
peanut mutter!

who takes me on da swimmin' trips from jersey to alabammy.....
mammy!

who gave me a sister when i had a daddy and two brothers.....
mother!

who puts the bandage on my hurts when I sprains my ankle like a dummy.....
mummy!

who cleans da doit from my doity shoit when i falls into da gudder.....
mudder!

who do I love da most in the roughsies and da calmsies.....
momsies!

*My spring semester of my first year of college was just
about over, so I wrote this to my mother. (1969)*

tonight i woke the pierced blinds
to seek a starry hue
the silence spoke in mute sighs
and spoke of nothing new
and thru the screen the moon shines
the sky is shadowed blue
a shadow in moon flute
some moment touched too few
it beckon seeking parted minds
two minds which one are few
finding a truth that love binds
it harbor i miss you

july 9

tonight i broke the pierced blinds

to seek a starry hue

the silence spoke in mute signs

and spoke of nothing new

and through the screen the moon shines

the sky is shadowed blue

a shaded wire prison finds

some moments touched, too few

it beckons seeking parted minds

those minds which one are two

fighting a truth love binds

it shouts how i miss you

On a summer night. (1969)

laughter include the word
  of every new day
  of every new night
laughter include the word

laughter include the day why
laughter to the sound wins cry

laughter include of breath
the first one of life,   the last of death

laughter reach up to truth
laughter include the word

... ... laughter ... ... and ...
did I laugh until to ... ...
... ...

even to tear and the pure splitting
into "... hole —
even it something ... ... that I love it
... ...
he ... like a ...
but laughter include the word
  laughter include the ...

laughter includes the word

laughter includes the word

of everyman's day
of everyman's night

laughter includes the word

laughter includes the breath

the first one of life
the last one of death

laughter searches for the truth
laughter includes the word

last night laughter found my heart
did i laugh with its smile
or did mine depart

was it tears and pain splitting
guts in my side,
was it something said that i heard,
god won't help me say
he knows it anyway

but laughter includes the word
laughter includes the word

After I was unfairly fired from a summer lumberyard job
in my sophomore year of college. (1969)

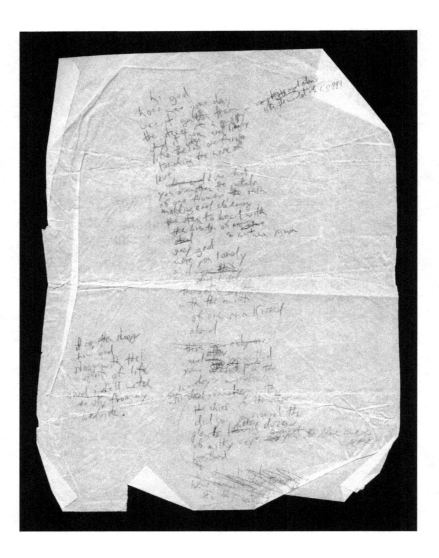

hi god, how was your day?

hi god,
how was your day?

was it gentler than the stance of a puppy?
did it loom and linger like the grace of one
finger touching the nose of love?

how did you strengthen the petals of one flower,
the rain molding and cleaning the stem to bend
with the breath of an autumn yawn?

say god,
were you lonely?

and did i see your thoughts
drifting with the mist
of one sun-kissed cloud?

and after you pulled your soft shade
on the day's window

did you jog around the planets
pitting dozens of milky ways
against the black awe of space?

and now will you sleep with the chirp
of the stars?

if so, then sleep now god

sleep with the spirit of life

and i shall watch the sky
from my bedside

*One summer evening in the attic, Lincoln Park, NJ, I woke about
1:00 am, looked out the window at the sky, wrote this, and went
back to sleep. (1969)*

inspector number eighteen

i should write something
upon this empty egg case
lying in the corner
of this rugless room

the box no longer collects eggs,
it does collect time though

much like a no-return bottle
of unbranded soda
or the empty chair where no one
ever sits in the dining room

this empty egg case
distributed by the brooklyn egg case company, incorporated
was inspected by inspector number eighteen.

inspector number eighteen
would have been
the president of the united states
had he not been shell-shocked in war

now he boxes shells

i wonder who inspected the eggs
i wonder if he is a friend
of inspector number eighteen

or, if the noble inspector is sitting
somewhere in a rugless room collecting time
for the brooklyn egg case company, incorporated

*In the heat of the Vietnam War I was a freshman at Syracuse University in
Parsons Cottage on campus with 30 other students. We were told we had to
move to a dormitory. We protested the move. One evening I was alone in
the main room of the cottage. Most of the furniture was gone. A large empty
egg box remained. I used the egg box as a makeshift writing desk. (1968)*

the coke bottle

erase the grease prints from the coke bottle my

lips melted the beach sands when i saw that

girl walking this way and somebody took

the bottle from my hand and gave me

the smudge of grease with rouge

lipstick and she smiled and

i smiled and i returned

a hope and she left

and i didn't at

all see her

anyway

no not

me:

!

The original was typed on my Olivetti typewriter. It took me hours to create the correct spacing—an allegory of the poem. (1970)

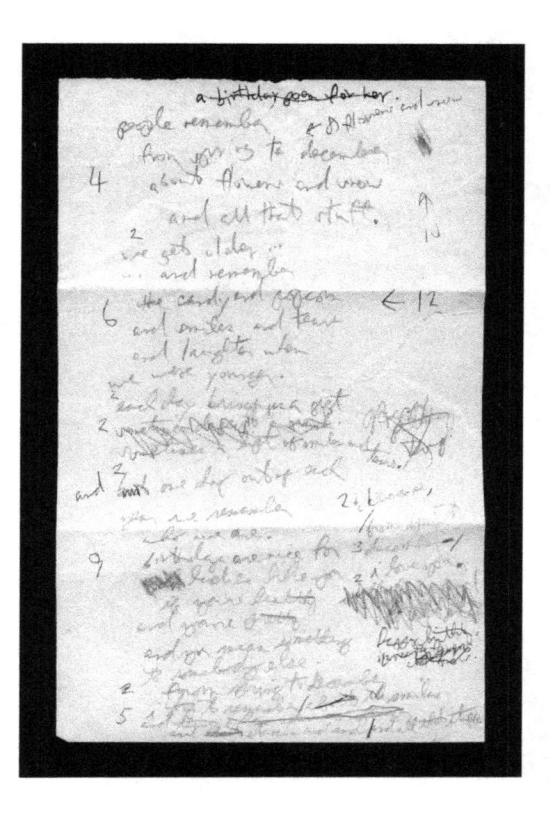

flowers and snow

people remember
from spring to december
about flowers and snow
and all that stuff

we get older
and remember
the candy and popcorn
and smiles
and tears
and laughter
when we were younger

each day brings us
a gift of smiles and tears

and one day
out of each year
we remember who we are

birthdays are nice for
ladies like you
if you're healthy
and you're pretty
and you mean something
to someone else

from spring to december
i try to remember
the smiles and tears
and flowers and snow
and all that stuff
because,
from spring to december
i love you

happy birthday

*For a girl I was dating, I never sent her the
poem because we broke up. (1970)*

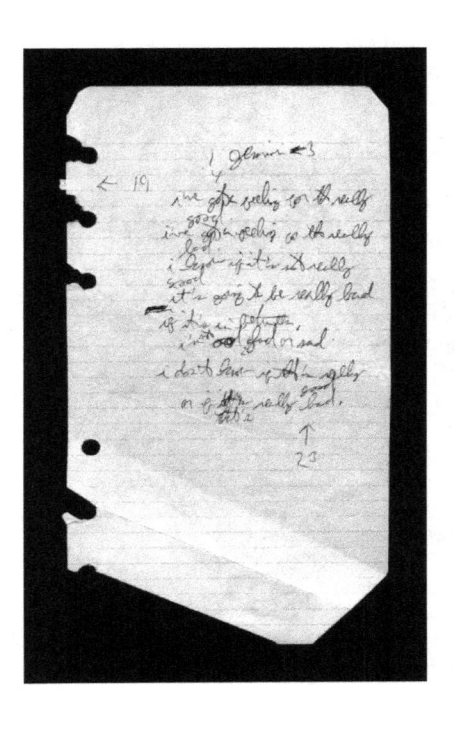

gemini

i've got a feeling for the really good

i've got a feeling for the really bad

i know if it's not really good,

it's going to be really bad

if it's in-between,

i'm not glad or sad

i don't know if that's really good

or if that's really bad

Being a Gemini is a lifelong struggle—gift or curse. (1970)

1 ↓ 8
4   requiem to eddie ~~scratch~~

he was a master of the gutter
his name was eddie
5 and his life
had been woven from
the neck of a bottle.
2

as a young man
he had seen the smile
in the sun.
and fun,
well,
eddie was also
10 a master of fun.
he knew that the art
of dancing was the souls
passage into another time.
2

he knew how to eat cheese
and how to sip wine.
4 eddie knew how to savor
the memory of a cool rain.
2
3 eddie's heart had been
touched with sweetness
and sadness.
2
he would burst into tears
4 at the sight of a fallen bird.
eddie had fell many times himself,
and once too hard.
2

eddie's life had been poignant
4 pieces of dream world
that had been scattered by
2 his own humility.

the master of the gutter
4 had drank too much whiskey
for one man.
2 and now he was dead.
1 eddie was a master of fun.

↑   6 6
6   5 4
     ——
      1 2

← 1⁷

requiem to eddie

he was a master of the gutter
his name was eddie
his life has been woven
from the rags of a bottle

as a young man
he had seen the smile in the sun,
and fun,
well,
eddie was also a master of fun

he knew the art of dancing
was the soul's passage into another time

he knew how to eat cheese
and how to sip wine

eddie knew how to savor
the memory of a cool rain

eddie's heart had been
touched with sweetness and sadness

he would burst into tears
at the sight of a fallen bird
eddie had fallen many times himself,
and once too hard

eddie's life had been poignant pieces of dream winds
scattered by his own humility

the master of the gutter
had drunk too much whiskey for one man
and now he was dead

eddie was a master of fun

*Eddie was my childhood friend's alcoholic dad. I remember how he cried
when he saw the bird lying on the street. He was holding a glass with ice
cubes and a dark liquid, presumably whiskey. (1970)*

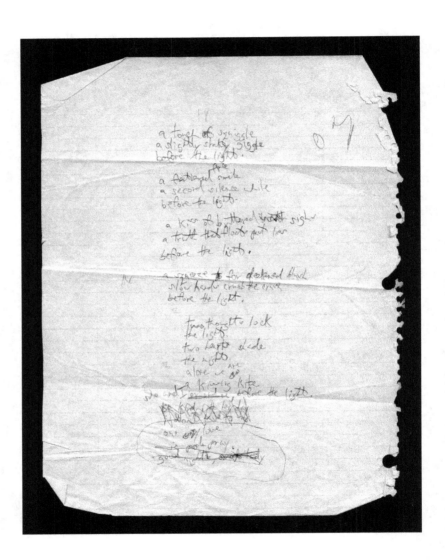

before the light

a touch of squiggle
a slightly shaky giggle
before the light

a feathered free smile
a second silence while
before the light

a kiss of buttered sighs
a truth that floats past lies
before the light

a squeeze for cheeky blush
slow hands crumble the crush
before the light

two thoughts lock
the light
two hearts shade
the night

alone we are,
a kissing kite

she and i,
before the light

Syracuse University in my room. (1971)

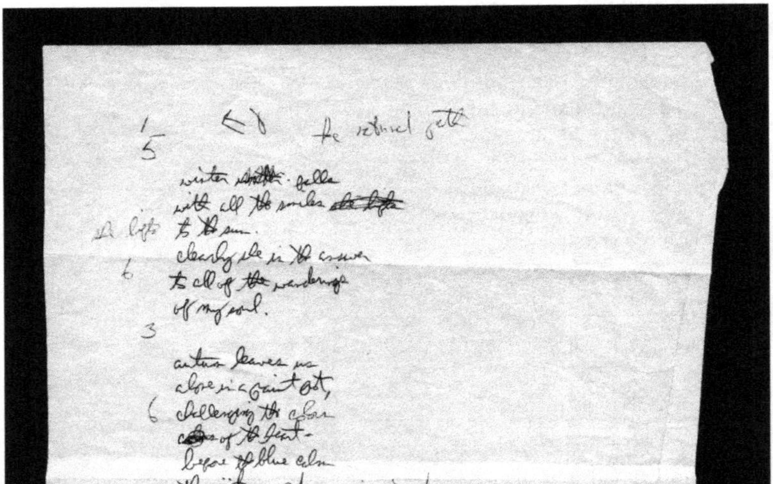

the natural path

summer sweats
every inch of our
rhythmic body music
the melted candle wine
bottle nestles into
a new form

fall leaves us
alone in a paint pot
challenging the colors
of the heart
before the blue calm
the spirit of us is fiery red

winter falls
with all of the smiles
she lifts to the sun
clearly she is the answer
to the wanderings
of my soul

spring is why all
newborn lovers look
back at the seasons
it is the natural path;
always behind their eyes
and in front of their hearts

About a relationship that didn't work out. (1971)

35 heartbeats

i've been trying to pulse
my life with friendship
and it seems humility gauges it,
sensitivity sweetens it,
and love keeps running it

A snowy day in my room at Syracuse University. (1971)

i like to rhyme

i like to rhyme

half the time,

and, when i do,

it sounds lousy

Maintaining an emotional, physical, and spiritual balance
at 21 can be difficult. (1971)

today

today i met a beautiful smile
it completed only one frame
it stunned in an inch but stayed for a mile
and i didn't even get her name

At the corner of University Avenue and Waverly Avenue,
Syracuse University. I never saw that smile again. (1971)

a child

a child
(god's piece of fudge)

smiled a sugar smile
only a christmas cookie

could appreciate

Walking along Waverly Avenue in the direction of my student housing on the Syracuse University campus. A mom with a stroller let me peek at her baby. The baby gave me the biggest and cutest baby smile I had ever seen up to that point. I wrote these lines in my room at Grover Cleveland dormitory. (1971)

and i want her

the white horizon
yawns and bends
covering the hills
with window pain glares,
blinding the peeping woodchucks,
putting everything to sleep,
and the snow falls

*In Massachusetts on a snowy morning at a friend's place after
learning a girlfriend wouldn't be able to see me that night. (1971)*

The rewards of pain are the sacrifices of life
turned gold. ~~But strong blood is red in the metal.~~
~~They are indestructible mountains that God only believes.~~
~~A person must~~ ~~bear his cross, must~~ ~~find the~~
~~the true vein of life through the~~ ~~the spiritual strings of men~~
~~The true vein of life. Pure depths and pride.~~

Many men ~~climb~~ a mirrored ladder and ~~find~~
themselves in ~~a~~ hell. It is the men who
~~guess~~ the ~~lessons~~ of ~~confident steps~~. Each step
appears to be correct long, now ~~faded~~

Others ~~engage the~~ long ascent with determination
and ~~content~~. ~~They ~~not only ~~to the ladder, with ~~ ~~into~~
but the ~~neglects~~ each strand. Each strand burns a ~~silver~~
~~melted~~ ~~into~~ collaboration and onto the golden crust.

~~For~~ ~~They~~ ~~people~~ climb a mountain ~~felt~~
~~we it~~ ~~And a few bits of~~ ~~below~~ ~~realize~~
that ~~the beauty of the~~ mountain is the top of the ~~ascent~~
So ~~They lift~~ ~~the~~ Lord again ~~They climb~~ burning gold
~~The rewards of pain are the conquest of life turned gold.~~

~~The flesh must heal~~ ~~and reveal again~~. The
~~might~~ scars seem unbearable the who the blindness of
~~for~~ the limitations into the clear sight of faith.

the rewards of pain

the rewards of pain are the sacrifices of life turned gold
these rewards are found in indestructible mountains that god only blesses
it is there where the true vein of life transfers the painful strivings of man
into pure dignity and pride

many men climb a mirrored ladder and find themselves in a velvet hell
it is these men who only see the fineness and toughness of a challenging step
each step appears as coarse hemp; never touched

other men engage their long ascent with determination and desire
they see not only the ladder with its unsteady twined steps
they negotiate each strand
each strand burns a lustered metal onto calloused skin
and forms a golden crust
the flesh must heal and heal again
the scars seem unbearable

it is these men who never climb a mountain 'til they are at the top of that mountain
and when they reach their pinnacle
they gaze below
and realize the strength of their mountain
is the strength of their character

so they lift their heads again

they wear the blindness of their limitations with the clear sight of faith
they climb a burning gold
they know the rewards of pain
are the sacrifices of life turned gold

*About to be commissioned a 2nd Lieutenant, I asked the platoon training
commander if I could pin this poem on the bulletin board in our squad
bay at Officer Candiidates School in Quantico, VA. He agreed. (1972)*

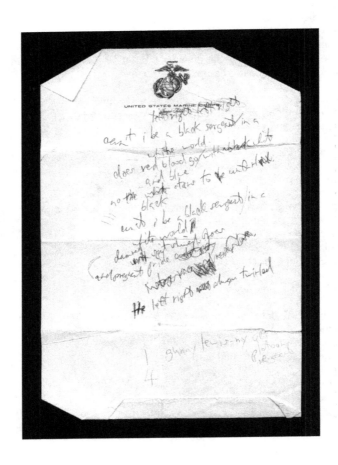

gunny lewis—my o.c.s. platoon sergeant

can't i be a black sergeant
in a white world?

does red blood go
with white and blue

no black stars to unfurl?

can't i be a black sergeant
in a white world?

damned spit-shined shoes
and pregnant pride

the left-right always twirled

During Officer Candidates School my gunnery sergeant taught me how to become "an officer and a gentleman." On one training day a few of the white candidates just weren't following his orders to his liking and he barked, "Can't I be a black sergeant in a white world?" (1972)

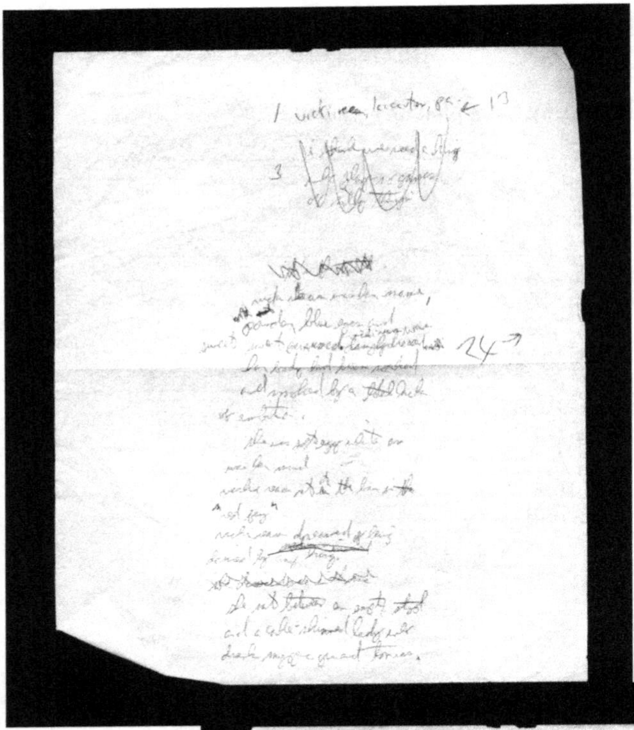

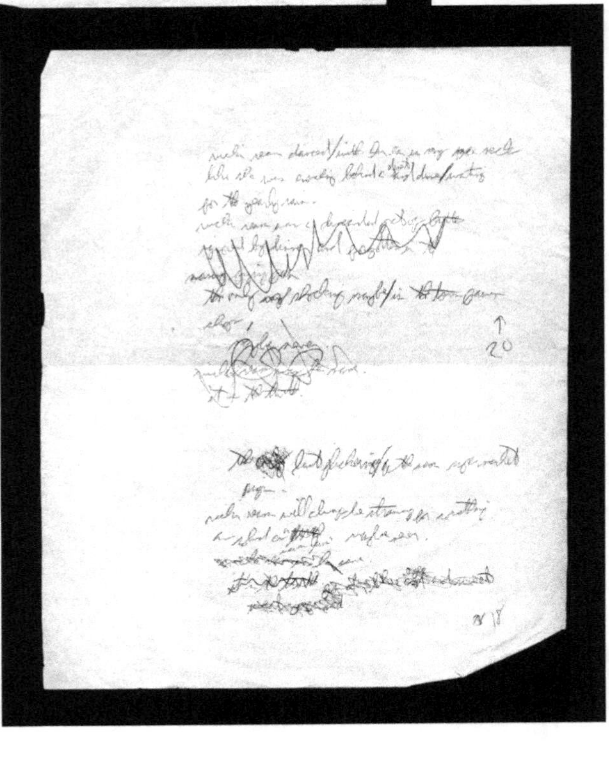

vicki reem, lancaster, pa.

vicki reem was her name,
powder-blue eyes and
sweet sweat perfumed,
vicki reem was damply dressed

her body had been soaked
and smoked by a total lack
of ambition

she was soft egg white
as was her mind
vicki reem sat at the bar
in the red fez
vicki reem dreamed of being
desired by any king

she sat between an empty stool
and a cake-skinned lady who
drank myopic gin and tonics

vicki reem danced
with her ear in my neck
as though she was crouching behind a desert sand dune
waiting for the yearly rain

vicki reem was the only living pledge
in the town pawn shop,
the last flickerings
of the neon supermarket sign

vicki reem will always strain for something
as solid as a warm kiss

maybe never

*On weekend leave from USMC Officer Candidates School with
an OCS friend. We stopped at a bar in Lancaster, PA. (1972)*

yes virginia, there is a jail

cold gut isolation
bars of twisted society
empty, shallow, and alone

tired walls, drooping, drowsy,
what a lousy life

tomorrow's boredom,
pale lights,
white lights,
day and night lights
staring at a neon cloud
that never crawls,
never bawls in the sky

wake up to breakfast,
the aluminum tin just
breaks the din for a
moment, a moment
empty, shallow, and alone

one crystal of salt
in an echoless stadium
never lifted by the wind

the quiet noise of the wooden bunk
hard and unbending,
life seems worthless
and so unending

eat the air
eat the night,
eat the day

why me

and, where is the sea?
i can't hear the sea!
i only hear the hollow flush
of the ragged toilets

echo empty,
echo shallow,
echo alone

i must get out!
please let me go!
i want to ride the wind!
and my spirit,
i still hear it
tho' my eyes are empty,
my breath is shallow,
my soul is alone,
alone, again, alone

After an unfortunate experience involving alcohol I was placed in jail overnight. (1972)

with my friends

we laughed at the pause

a silent applause,

there was no real cause

it was love

With Gary, Donna, Jim, Rick, and Gretchen in a bar in Batavia, New York. We always are happy to see each other. At one point there was a long silence. We laughed. We knew we were friends for life. (1974)

wB and iL

the warmth of myself/can never be heated –
⌐only caressed
⌐   ⌐ angel god, thank you
⌐the eyes of my soul/can never be damned –
⌐only blessed
⌐   ⌐ angel god, thank you
⌐the want of my heart/will never be isolated –
⌐it smiles in my breast
⌐   ⌐ thank you
⌐angel god, thank you

the warmth of myself

the warmth of myself
can never be heated,

only caressed,

angel god, thank you

the yes of my soul
can never be damned

only blessed,

angel god, thank you

the want of my heart
will never be isolated

it smiles in my breast

thank you

angel god, thank you

*During a period when I needed to trust myself
and trust in things I didn't understand. (1973)*

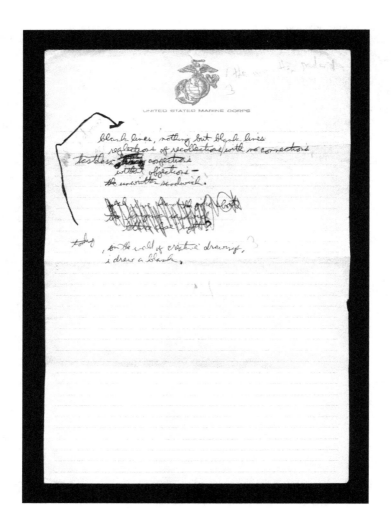

UNITED STATES MARINE CORPS

blank lines, nothing but blank lines
realizations of recollections/with no corrections
tasteless corrections
without objections –
the unwritten sandwich.

today, in the world of creative drawing,
i drew a blank.

48

the unwritten sandwich

today
in the world of creative drawings
i drew a blank

i drew blank lines,
nothing but blank lines

all reflections of recollections
with no connections
tasteless confections
without objections,

the unwritten sandwich
says so much

On one of those days when nothing worked. (1973)

i feel fat tonight, dammit
beef strogonoff will put me on
a diet of carrots and celery

and those noodles, oodles and oodles
of crispy noodles, ooh what foodles

but, that's it, no more for me
i'm tough, enough, enoff, onoff,
gonoff, oh gonoff
i'm strong enough to stay away, today
i'm really strogenough to stay away, today
dammit, i can't get enough of beef strogonoff

i feel fat tonight

i feel fat tonight, dammit
beef stroganoff will put me on
a diet of carrots and celery

and those noodles, oodles and oodles
of crispy noodles, ooh what foodles

but, that's it, no more for me
i'm tough, enough, enoff, onoff,
gonoff, oh ganoff
i'm really strong enough to stay away, today
i'm really strogenough to stay away, today
dammit, i can't get enough of beef stroganoff

Not feeling good about myself—undisciplined and sloppy. (1973)

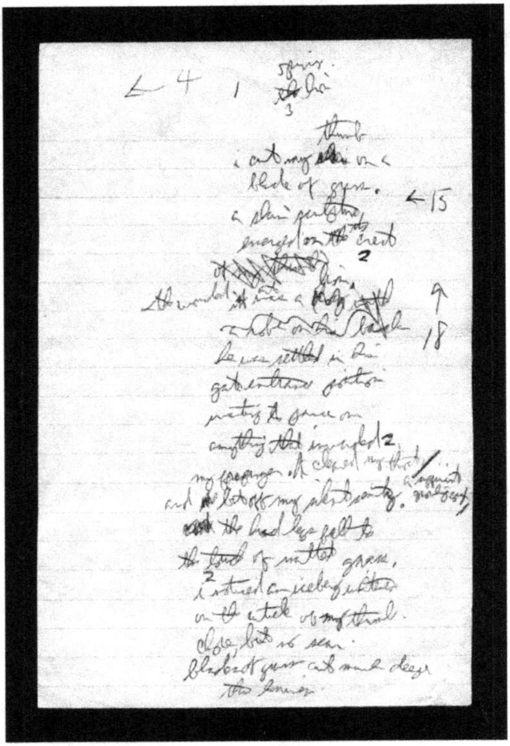

spring lion

i cut my thumb
on a blade of grass

a skin sculpture
emerged on its crest
the wounded art was a lion

he was settled in his
gate entrance position
waiting to pounce on
anything that invaded
my forefinger

i cleared my throat,
a sufficient growling cough,
and bit off my silent sentry
the hind legs fell to
the touch of matted grass

i noticed an iceberg whiteness
on the cuticle of my thumb
close, but no scar

blades of grass cut much deeper
than knives

*In the spring after falling on the ground
sliding with my palms down. (1973)*

3

edward g. played 'a' to 'z'
                    see!?

he never ketdup in his life
in them thirties and sixties,
                    or wife.
                    see!?

that artist of art
ran more through his heart —
through the film —

his hand was dark
            and soft.

a rennaissance man.

simply black and white
moves truth in night.

he died, and we lose him.

"no, you dummy, the trees
have lost you."
                    see?

on the passing of edward g. robinson

edward g. played "a" to "z",

"see?"

he never was held up in his life.
from those thirties to sixties,
or his wife,

"see?"

that artist of art
ran more through his heart,
through the film

i met him one noon

his hand was dark
and soft

a renaissance man

simply black and white
moreso truth in night

he died, and we lose him

"no, you dummy, the trees
have lost you"

"see?"

*Written the day of his passing. I had met Edward G. Robinson
on Park Avenue in New York City in the summer of 1969. When
he came out of a cab and walked in my direction, I extended my
hand and told him I admired his movie work. He engaged my
hand, thanked me, smiled, and kept walking down the street.
The quotes are from two of his movies. (1973)*

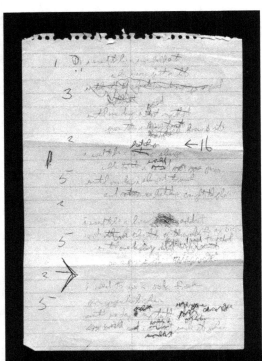

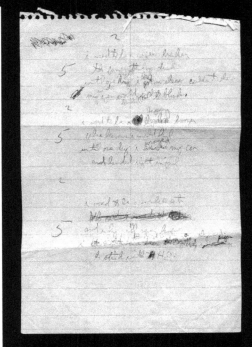

i used to be a snowball eater

i used to be a snowball eater
when i was just a tot,
until one day my throat so sore,
from then i knew to not

i used to be a ketchup slurper
whole bottles i would pour,
until one day i slurped too much
and ketchup caught the floor

i used to be a bosco addict
rich chocolate for my brain,
until one day i limped to school
on a pure milk sugar cane

i used to be a soda freak
from ginger ales to cokes,
until one day my teeth got sick
i couldn't smile at jokes

i used to be a coffee breaker
the famous thinking drink,
until one night i couldn't sleep
my wide eyes failed to blink

i used to a be a happy boozer
false heavens i would hail,
until one day i wronged my car
and landed right in jail

i used to be a snowball eater
and why, i'll never know,
i think it was skyward sign
to stick with H_2O

In a room in Olongapo City, Philippines,
while serving in the Marines. (1973)

tired nights tomorrow
awaken faintly sorrowed.
it would have been much nicer
if she smiled
let herself be captured by the
softening screen of the
lit ~~buzzing~~ bed

shared my love on your hair
beckoning for want
of one unwrinkled moment
of undamned spirit love.

today awaken~
tired nights to morrow.

tired night tomorrow

tired night tomorrow
awakened freshly sorrow

it would have been much nicer
if she had smiled
and let herself be captured
by the patterned screen
of my shining eye

shine my love on your hair

beckoning for want
of one unsimpled moment
of undamned purist love

today awakened
tired night tomorrow

*One morning in Okinawa in my room after an unusually
weary and complicated relationship ended. (1973)*

philippines hill

sitting on this hill
i see paintings
of other hills
and large waters

i see dark green
spider legs,
impacted fossil veins
of pre-historic grandeur
crawling up scaping
mountain noses

small puddles from
the waterbug
ships scratch
a wrinkled ocean

here,
small things bend
the edge of heaven

god speaks in
a clear voice

eternity begins

found on this hill
is found the waters
all painted by the sky

Atop a hill. My platoon was bivouacked below after a 25-mile
forced march. I walked up the hill, approximately 300 feet,
and looked out. (1974)

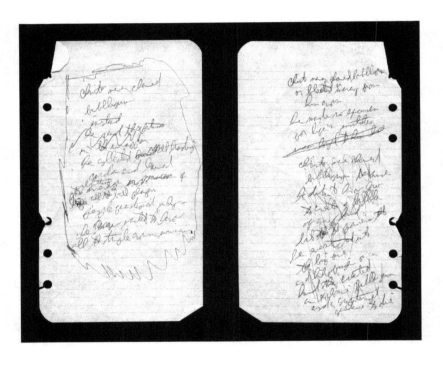

christ never chewed bubblegum

christ never chewed bubblegum

or bleated for mercy
from his cross

he made no excuse for
life's mistakes

christ never chewed bubblegum

instead,

he collected trading cards
and learned the batting averages
of all the ballplayers

people questioned why

he wanted to know
all the triple crown winners

Raised as a Roman Catholic, the concept of the father, the son, and the
holy ghost was and still is a mystery to me. Easter Sunday and opening
day for the Yankees are always just a few days apart. (1974)

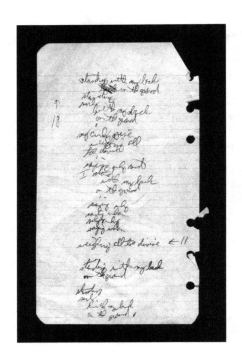

standing with my back on the ground

standing with my back
on the ground
standing
surly
with my back
on the ground

my curly spine
weighing all
too divine

saying why must
i stand
with my back
on the ground

saying why
saying when
saying why
saying when

weighing all
too divine

standing with my back
on the ground
standing
surly
with my back
on the ground

*With my infantry platoon in the northern training area in
Okinawa at the end of a 25-mile forced march with my infantry
platoon I stood as the officer while my Marines rested and
drank lots of water. I wrote this standing. I was an exhausted
"leader of men" and wanted to crumble to the ground. (1974)*

captain oliver north

a man who says
of another man,

"he is my idol"

must be idle himself

*Many years before he became a public figure, Captain Oliver North was
a respected officer in the U.S. Marine Corps. I received instruction from
him in 1972 at Officer Candidates School (OCS). Then again, in 1974,
he was one of my training officers in Okinawa. He had just instructed
three other 2nd Lieutenants and me in field leadership for serving our
infantry platoons. The other officers referred to the captain as their idol.
My interpretation of the captain's words was different. He was instructing
us to lead as unique individuals. I found a piece of paper and a stubby
pencil to record my thoughts at the time. (1974)*

saturday night television — cowboy

MR. 45

HELMET

riding my horse into the setting tube
i hadn't shaved today,
old seegah smoke fell on my face
i wartished in glass
riding my pony saddack ponies
while eating bologna and drinking a beer
from the rear of the living room

riding my horse into the setting tube
i stood sweaty and jostley
on straddling my armchair saddle
i was herding cattle
while rounding the mustard
crowed the crust of my mustard meal

riding my horse into the setting tube
i pulled on my reins

i was loser than coffee brown mud
drifting through the bad town in my suds
with in a back bending bump
i terminated my eyes
and gently to sleep,

dozed off

1
3
9
2
9
<
9
35
15
3
15

saturday night television cowboy

riding my horse into the setting tube
i hadn't shaved today.
old screen "seegah" smoke felt good
on my face
i was right in my place
riding my pony
while eating a bologna sandwich
and pouring a beer
from the rear of the living room

riding my horse into the setting tube
i sat sweat-cooled leathered.
arms straddling my
armchair saddle
i was herding cattle
while rounding up
the mustard
around the crust
of my spice-soaked bread

riding my horse into the setting tube
i pulled on my reins
i was looser than coffee-ground mud
drifting nice
in my suds
when, in a back-bending burp
i wiped out wyatt earp
and dozed off
gently to sleep

*I was thinking about my father watching a western on a black
and white TV. He enjoyed his beer and a sandwich. (1974)*

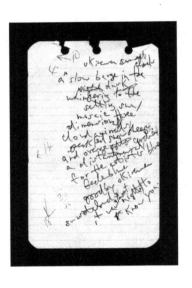

okinawa sunset clouds

a slow barge in the dusk

whimpering to the setting sun

mosaic three-dimensional

cloud animals,

sparkled snow sheep,

and orange cotton candies

a distant mural

for the artist's blue

fade blue

goodbye, okinawa

sunset clouds

it was almost nights

to know you

On a plane above Okinawa heading toward the US
for my next tour of duty in the Marine Corps. (1974)

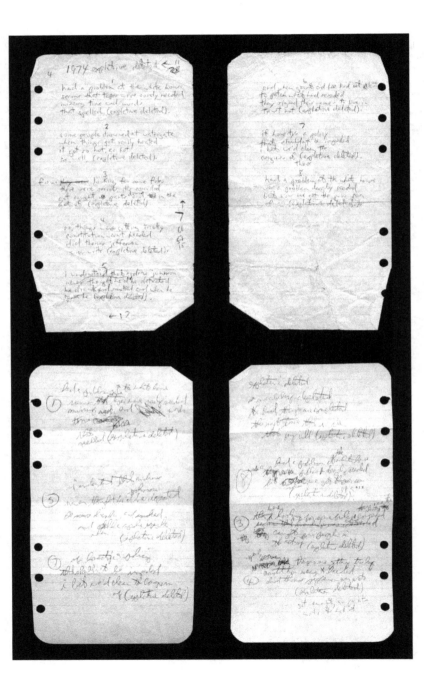

expletive deleted (august 10)

had a problem at the white house
seems that tapes were sorely needed,
missing time and words
that spelled (expletive deleted)

some people drowned at watergate
when things got really heated,
it got so hot, as hot
as, well (expletive deleted)

four looking for some files
there were secrets, it's conceded,
got caught, pants down, and in the
act of (expletive deleted)

so, things were getting tricky
constitution wasn't heeded,
did thomas jefferson
ever write (expletive deleted)

i understand andrew johnson
thought he'd never be defeated,
he drank and smoked and when he
spoke he (expletive deleted)

and when grant and lee had met at last
to patch what had seceded,
they signed their names to live in
trust, not (expletive deleted)

if honesty's a policy
that shouldn't be impeded,
i bet we'd clean the
congress of those (expletive deleted)

had a problem at the white house
was a problem deeply seated,
but now we got the poor son
of a (expletive deleted)

The day after President Nixon resigned. (1974)

sleeping champions

spaced apart like rundown toys
and placed like monopoly figures along shine-tiled avenues
where wheel-barrowed old ladies in pink dresses wear hair in pink curlers
that sets all wet all day

where dignity dies

on the elevator, sweepers
and week-old bearded floor aides
share brooms
with the last breaths
of a supine old white man

the old white man wonders
if the inertia from the lift
is really the first step to heaven
or the last reality of hell

half-beamed and coal-eyed he speaks,
"are you going to secaucus, buddy?
I need a ride to secaucus"

this is the place where the ancient, antique ones
shrivel with the best possible care
where puréed diets
make puréed bowel movements
for puréed minds
where dignity dies

where crying is as normal as staring at a wall
for twelve hours a day
where muzak melts into soiled sheets
where everyone is a sleeping champion

and so, at last, the old white man returns to a distance
with rosaries in his brains
and blotched skin stains
his hair is silver sparse
life is no longer a farce
for him dignity dies

While working for a hospital supply company.
One of my accounts was a nursing home. (1975)

← 10 the breeze

4

(the accumulation of all the breezes produces
a tender wind ~~that~~ sun may warm for a warm
may ~~night~~ day.
severed from the blue sky/sky the rain will
~~delights~~ seep into the ~~earth~~ earth.
no stones for children
~~why~~ reincarnates ~~trees~~ for boys/low turtles
in the young.   anguish, escape it out.
one tree ~~feed~~ of yours
and the ~~damn~~ green leaves
or very ~~making~~ explosive
to the ~~breeze~~.
the breeze,   ~~anguish pour it out~~
carried ~~so loud~~ by the ~~feet~~ of a child's
~~pulse~~
the breeze,/nature's pulse so real!
the breeze/
the almighty breeze of life,/

the breeze

the accumulation of all the breezes
produces a tender wind
the sun may warm
for a warm may night

severed from the blue cloud sky
the raindrops dance with the breeze

no storms for children

reincarnation bears slow turtles in the spring

pine trees yawn

dawn brings green leaves
on young saplings
responsive to the breeze

the breeze,
caressed by the heat of a child's smile

the breeze,
nature's pulse for seed

the breeze,
the almighty sneeze of life

A spring day in Lincoln Park, NJ. (1975)

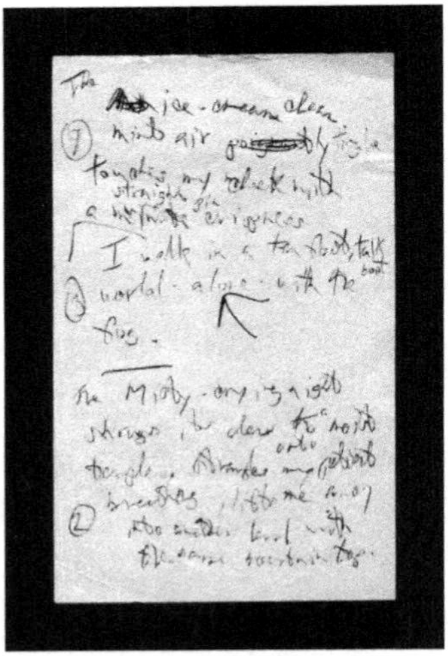

the fog

the ice cream clean mint air
tingle touches my cheek
with a straight-pin crispness

the misty crying night shrugs
its dew onto my moist temple,
strangles my patient breathing,
lifts me away into another land

with the same mountain top

i walk in a ten-foot world
I talk through my boots aswirl

alone,
with the fog

*After an early evening spring walk, unusually heavy fog was on the
ground and the boots I wore sounded out the steps I should take. (1975)*

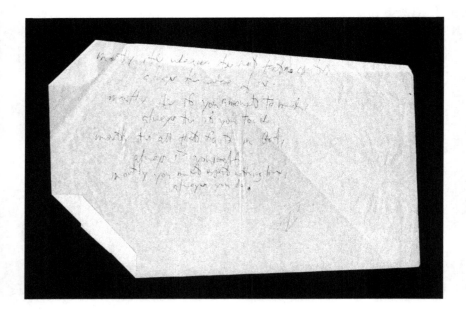

mostly always

mostly it's where it's not that counts;

always it's where it is

mostly it's if you amount to much;

always it's if you touch

mostly you must expect nothing less;

always you do

mostly it's all that faith in god;

always it's you

At my third floor walk-up apartment in Clifton, NJ,
while attending graduate school. (1975)

we all must wait sometimes

we all must wait sometimes
we wait for words and rhymes
we wait for heaven or hell
Knowing that even friends can't tell.

we all must park sometimes
we bite the struggling climbs
we stand in queues we don't
Knowing hope is hard to trust

we all must love sometimes
we love to see that shines
we wait, ~~however the sun~~
we're strong, we seek the sun.

we all must wait sometimes

we all must wait sometimes
we wait for words and rhymes
we sit for heaven or hell
knowing even friends can't tell

we all must hate sometimes
we hate the struggling climbs
we stand in rooms of dust
knowing hope is hard to trust

we all must love sometimes
we love to see what shines
we wait, we never run
we're strong, we seek the sun

Between military service and graduate school on a summer day. (1975)

a word or two

a word or two
about the smile
i gained one day
from a stylish looking chick

it wasn't hard for me
to pick the time of day,
or otherwise
the lovely doll wore
no disguise

the day wore lovely
roses bloomed
the smile she wore
was soft perfumed

if i had worn
no worse for where
i wonder if her smile'd be there,
i wonder if she'd animate,
i wonder if i'd palpitate

i wonder,
do you wonder too
to see a smile that just a few
can pray for
at any time

the difference 'tween
lemon and lime

you must agree the
eyes of mime

are simply held in
place of time

and time and time again
i'll see her smile when when is when

*On a warm spring day and a chance encounter with
a well-dressed lady who smiled at me. (1975)*

84

quitting time

the last drift had fallen for the day
when the night started its hum for the dawn,
now all who wanted to would pray
and the king of the world would think of the pawn

pieces of darkness developed from the naked air
sliding between the curtain showers,
wrinkled smiles came to bear
the plastered walls passed out for hours

quitting time
is a fitting time
to relax

*My first job after military service was an unhappy experience
for me. I couldn't wait for the work day to be over. (1975)*

1

she has my eyes
she has my smile
she knows i want
her to stay for a while.
she know i need her
breath to kiss,
she know i need her love
i want to give her all
my love. i want to
speak with her,
but i don't have to
she has my eyes.
she has my smile.

2

her eyes [pretty]
her mouth.
her [blanket] mouth
which gently
melts my tear
she gazing at
me after til the tears
join the clouds in
the sky.

2

she wants me to be happy
she warms her joy

she
a wrecked kitten
playing tiger

2
she gives me sweetness. 28
i love her.
she knows
she has my eyes
she has my smile

she has my eyes

she has my eyes, she has my smile
she knows i want her to stay a while
she knows i need her breath to kiss,
she knows i need her love
i want to give her all my love
i want to speak with her,
but i don't have to,
she has my eyes
she has my smile

she wants me to be happy
she swarms her joy

she,
a nuzzled kitten
playing tiger
she gives me that sweetness

i love her
she knows
she has my eyes
she has my smile

For Diane. (1976)

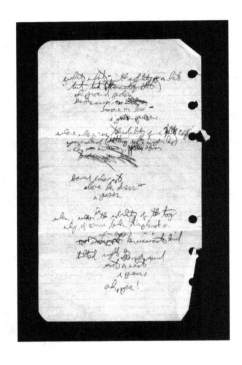

the nobility of a hat

what, what,
is the nobility of a hat

tut, tut,
it's exactly that
oh, proud fedora,
embracing more or less,

i guess

where, where,
is the nobility of a cap

yes, indeed,
setting right in your lap

ah, autumn cover,
bowed below, not above her dress,

i guess

when, when,
is the nobility of the top

why, of course,
when it's placed on your crop
an inanimate kind,
tilted right on your mind, east or west,

i guess

ah, yes

After seeing three different men on Madison Avenue
wearing three different hats. (1976)

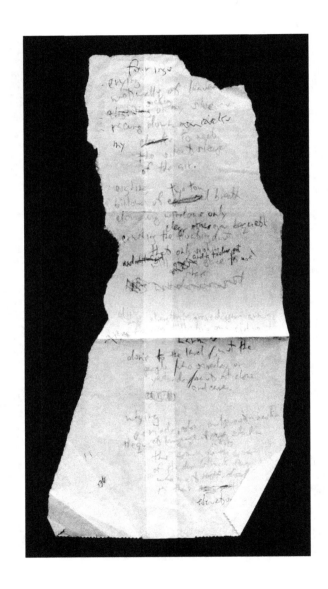

four ings

crying

wet walls of leaves
soaking on my sleeves

racing out of my mind
and down my cheeks
waiting for the painless jump
to meet the silent sleep of the air

sighing

billows of two-ton breath
clouding windows clear eyes bequeath

crushing the floating dust
only sighing
and a timeless pit
will space and share

dying

only strengthens gravediggers arms
the farmer tills his own and no harm is

done to the land
just the people
who someday or yesterday
must sit alone and care

whying

periods, colons, and question marks
the quiet language of inking sharks

the comma is the coma
for the dumbstruck few
who wait half dead
in their elevator lair

Feeling isolated and alone trying to put meaningful words on paper. (1976)

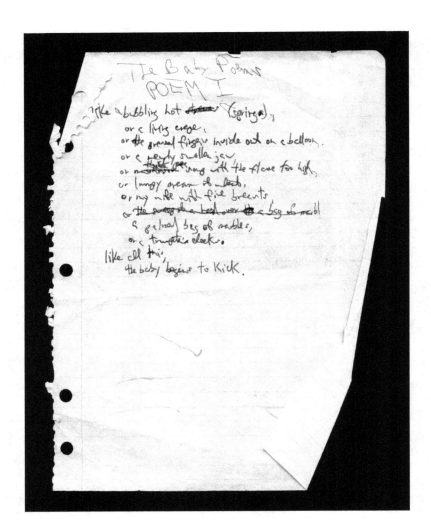

The Baby Poems
POEM I

like a bubbling hot ~~spring~~ (spring),
   or a living eye,
   or the ~~grand~~ finger inside out on a balloon.
   or a newly swollen jaw
   or ~~~~ ~~song~~ with the flame too high,
   or lumpy cream to ~~back~~,
   or my wife with five breasts,
   or the ~~~~ ~~bend over~~ a bag of ~~marble~~
      a pained bag of marbles,
   or a tomato clock.

like all this,
   the baby begins to kick.

like a bubbling hot spring

like a bubbling hot spring

or a living crêpe of strawberries

or pressed fingers inside out on a balloon

or a newly swollen jaw

or pea soup with the flame too high

or lumpy cream of wheat

or my wife with five breasts

or a palmed bag of marbles

or a trumpeter's cheeks

like all this,

the baby begins to kick

Diane was pregnant with Renée. We were both
fascinated by the movement in her belly. (1979)

he fell on my shoulder
like a crepe suzette boulder
his eyes ~~firm white~~ and cute
like ~~his eyes~~ me blueberry fruit
he needed ~~I~~ growing
or ~~me~~ no/to time
~~like~~ a ~~crinkled~~ pillow
his shoulder was mine.
we had been out ~~past~~ ~~the night~~ him
~~and his hair had been~~ ~~since~~ by day
~~get out~~ of the backseat
i picked up the strange

little boy moved like
his hand moved like
a sleeping ~~ghost~~ note
now he lay on his face.
my ~~wife~~ and i want to sleep
as my ~~one year~~ rolled over
~~~~ to the ~~top~~ of the night
he's only six months older than the light.
~~but~~ ~~and~~ he'll smile ~~in~~ the light.

he fell on my shoulder

he fell on my shoulder
a crêpe suzette boulder
his eyes slit cute
like blueberry fruit

no mention of evening
or mention of time
an animated pillow
his shoulder was mine

out past eight
for him, a big change
out of the backseat
I picked up the strange little boy

his hands moved
like a sleeping puppet

now he lay in his crib

my wife and I went to sleep

as our son rolled over
to the tune of the night

he's six months old
he will smile when it's light

Back from a family event with our son, Ryan. (1979)

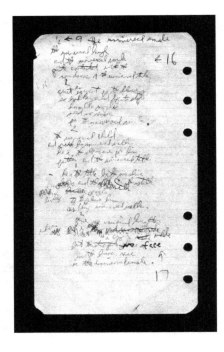

the universal smile

the universal laugh
and the universal smile

quite contented with
the roundness
of the universal tile

quite in earnest
for the blessings
so emblazoned by its style

humble people
need no reason
for the universal smile

the universal child
and the universal walk
is the showcase for the father
and the universal talk

is the table by the sunshine
and the gold shine on the stalk
living people
try to please him
never tempted to bemock

give me universal laugher
when i sigh, I think awhile

but the strongest face
in the human race
is the universal smile

Our two babies, two years apart, were being served
breakfast. They were happy though the morning news
delivered at the end of the driveway was not. (1980)

the english channel ran clear
and the river way

1
3

i split the water for
a quarter of a dream
and start my legs in
a rectangular stream.
i've swam and swam
in all the dynamics and
i've picked my own tarzan
flick, made love to jane,
then swam around the corner
to find other beautiful legs
and flat bellies without faces
dreamily changing as i gasp
my spaces and flip my turns.
my fingers touch the channels edge
and as i listen to the music
of the water my heart beats
its easy stroke.
in the noontime i'm a wave in and out
of women and bobbing children
in a dance we learned along playing
in the reflection of the day.
no one is as happy as i.

98

the channel swimmer

i split the water for a quarter of a dream
and start my laps in a rectangular stream

i swim in all the olympics,
and star in my own tarzan flick (saving jane)

then swim around the corner
to find beautiful legs
and fat bellies without faces
eternally changing
as i gasp my races
and flip my turns

my mind flips too,
the channels churn,
as i listen to the music of the water
my heart beats louder with every stroke

in the noontime
i weave in and out
among mommies and bobbing children

i'm a dancer on a flooded floor
flying in the reflection of the sky

no one is as happy as i

After a July swim at the Lincoln Park Swim Club, Lincoln Park, NJ. (1985)

images the soft vigor of night

my image of you is an unshelled whip
shifting with the ease on the soft vigor of night and
the permanent ~~sense~~ contained in sight
of a star's beauty.
cast us darkly within our smiles,
weave the grain of faith,
powder our breathing air with our own faith.
power the notion of togetherness thru the night.
grasp our earnest whispers
drink moistly the soft vigor of night in that
the soft vigor of night may bring us understanding.

11·14·78

the soft sips of night

my image of you
is an unshelled ship
shifting with sleep waves
on the soft sips of night

and the permanent contained insight
of a star's beauty

cast us darkly with our smiles
upon the soft sips of night,
sieve the grains of faith
powder our breathing air
with our own faith

power the motion of togetherness
through the night

grasp our earnest whispers

drink moistly the soft sips of night,
the soft sips of night
will bring us understanding

For my wife, Diane. (1988)

                    like a bunch of dole bananas
like a bunch of dole bananas/sitting on the frigdge
or the space between the arches/ of the verrasano brideg
i'v impressed myself with my sweeping self
and have come to realize i will sit on the shelf longer
than the fruit,
or perish my ambitions
and sit on top of my sink
→ longer the the seal of approval,
writing my own good housekeeping seal of approval
waiting forever to be picked by the world
as the best taste in town
like a bunch of dole bananas sitting on the fridge
waiting forever to be known as the space between the
arches of the verrazano brief bridge
is am only the a straw in the broom
eventually to be broken off to become part of the swept
residue, of a cleaning proces.
eaten to exist,
like the space between the arches of a dole banana bridge.

like a bunch of dole bananas

like a bunch of dole bananas sitting on the fridge
or the space between the arches of the verrazano bridge,
i've impressed myself with my sweeping self
and have come to realize I could sit on the shelf longer than the fruit
and perish my ambition down the chute
waiting longer than a seal of approval,
my own good-housekeeping seal of approval,
waiting forever to be picked by the world as the best taste in town

like a bunch of dole bananas sitting on the fridge
or the space between the arches of the verrazano bridge,

a straw in the broom to become part of the swept residue

like the space between the arches of a dole banana bridge

*At the kitchen table in Montville, NJ, while gazing at
a bunch of bananas on top of the refrigerator. I was
thinking about the NYC Marathon I ran in 1978. (1995)*

i love the dark rain
when green shoes
and the sun is blinded
by the clouds.
the sky grumbles, then
and bellies,
but i can smell i
the dark rain

love of all the color
that god has created
on the earth,
sensing light
i have loved the dark rain.

i love the dark rain
when crisp met
and golden corn beneath
my toes
the earth mountain flush
and shrink
and leaves drink
the dark rain

so the sky to
smell my teeth
i have loved the dark rain.

i love the dark rain

i love the dark rain
where green shines
and the sun is blinded by the clouds

the sky grumbles, talks and balks,
and I can walk in the dark rain
free of all the pains
god has created for the earth

since my birth
i have loved the dark rain

i love the dark rain
when air is sweet
and puddles form beneath my toes

the mountain mud stumbles,
blinks and shrinks
and my eyes drink the dark rain
imprisoned by the joy
god has created for the earth

since my birth
i have loved the dark rain

At our home in Montville, NJ, after walking
barefoot in a muddy backyard. (1995)

LBI Sunrise 7/20/02 6:06 AM

vers II

orange candy ball,
resting silhouette gulls
on the swaying water stage.
a parade of breeze gold sea dust
widening the pathway linking, to
clapping ripples
a moist butterfly carpet.
the captain warming, three legged wandering
imprints marching in to circle of dune
cool toes
all desire to roll forward crystal jewelry
foams without the vehicles yet the grace
of the breeze crossing my back
how the hue spread out over
the tiny golden back of every roof.
my stomach finally ground
the time to return the favor
to bring this joy back from the waterage.

lbi sunrise (6:06 am april 20)

orange candy ball,
resting silhouette gulls
on the swaying water stage

a mirage of banana-gold sea dust
widening the pathway,
linking light to clapping ripples,
a moist butterfly carpet

the eastern morning

three-legged wandering imprints
marching in the dune's inclination

cool toes

all decisions roll forward, roll forward, roll forward
shell jewelry forms a necklace
with the grace of the sea breeze around me

how the hue grasps and grows
the fiery golden heart of every welcoming roof
warming the tones inside

my shadow finally appears
the time to return the favor arrives,
to bring this joy
from the oceanscape
to my resting woman

*On Brant Beach, 53rd Street, Long Beach
Island, NJ, early one morning. (2002)*

Black Tie Affair # 13/12/07

perhaps,
it was the angle of my chair
or the softness in your air
quieting with my face at this fireplace,
reaching to mind whatever said.
but you were sitting behind my head
I wanted you, to take to bed.

Your elbow holding my neck like feet
upon a misty deck
caressing, holding grace at this fireplace
You laughed the myself up to warm yourself
and I relaxed, and then looked up
still forward to the words up front.
You told me on a bike for two
And something that I always knew
We rested on these guided chairs
were yours of gentle, strengthened love.

you laughed again
and smiled
and listened well,
the podium was talking tall
but we no one had heard the bell
touching corners, our two seats
touching hearts, that wait next
you our reclined eight legged like.
Lord to decide,
most wouldn't care

you and me and a fir chair
black tie affair
c very nice

A Common Health Company

black tie affair (at the plaza hotel, new york city)

perhaps
it was the angle of my chair,
or the softness in your hair
pointing with my face,
at this plaza place,
feigning mind
at what was said

there you sat,
behind my head
i wanted you
to take to bed

your elbow found my shoulder and neck
like feet upon a misty deck,
caressing, molding space,
at this plaza place

you laughed,
then snuggled up to warm yourself
and I relaxed, and then looked up
still forward to the words up front

you held me on a bike for two
and something that I always knew,
that rested on these gilt-edged chairs
were years of gentle, strengthened love

you laughed again and smiled
and listened well,
the podium was talking tell
but we as one had heard the bell

touching corners, our two seats
touching hearts, which wait then meet
upon our cushioned eight-legged bike

hard to describe,
most wouldn't care,
you and i,
each on a chair
a very sweet black-tie affair

*Diane and I attended a charity dinner at the Plaza Hotel in
NYC. She was sitting close to me. I wrote this on the back
of the dinner invitations during the presentations. (2003)*

silly is good

silly is silly
and silly is good

silly is happy
and misunderstood

silly is funny
and foolish, and yes,
silly is the best part
of cleaning a mess

silly is wild
and silly is crazy
silly is tame
and silly is lazy

you being silly
doesn't mean you are bad
your mind is just wandering
maybe more than a tad

silly is playing with
what is not known
silly is best
in crowds or alone

you being silly
doesn't mean you're insane
you've loosened your smile
and relaxed your whole brain

silly is instant and silly is quick
silly is healthy and good when you're sick

you being silly
means your heart has been lifted
from rainy to sunny
silly has shifted

though serious things can cause people strife
add a touch of silly and you'll lighten your life

At home in Montville, NJ, after being "accused" of being a silly man by Diane. (2005)

noisy pants, squeaky shoes!

noisy pants, squeaky shoes,
walking down the hall,
what's the link to how they think
do they think i'll fall?

noisy pants, squeaky shoes,
walking all day long,
is the sound on the ground,
just a running song?

does each boot
try to root
for each leg to hum?

does each stride
stretch and glide
to a beating drum?

does each sock
like to rock
to music for my toes?

do my laces
form strange faces
all tied up in prose?

noisy pants, squeaky shoes,
singing in the rain,
will a sprinkle, make a wrinkle
on my pants again?

noisy pants, squeaky shoes,
the rain has stopped, I'm pleased!

thanks so much,
what's this I hear?
oh no, my creaking knees!

*At my first book festival in NYC waiting for anyone
to buy the first copy of my first book. (2008)*

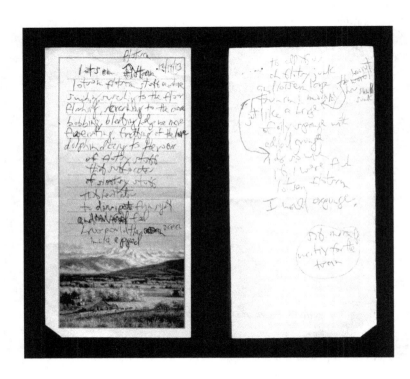

lotsam flotsam

lotsam flotsam stuff on shore
swishing, swashing, salty floor

flashing, scrashing to the core
bobbing, bleating, "help me, more!"

feasting, fretting of the lore
dolphin dazing to the roar

of flotsy stuff
that suffocates
of slooty stuff
that hesitates

disintegrates
from sight and feel
how could the ocean make appeal

to all of us

oh flotsy junk
and lotsam large
the worst has sunk
just like a barge

of oily sponge
tsunami mommy
adding grunge

i so do wish
if I were fish

lotsam flotsam
I would expunge

I was waiting for a subway. I saw trash on the tracks. I thought
of the ocean. We are all part of the ocean. (2013)

this is a type-writer and it seems to be working well.
and that would be a single space.

and that would be a double space.

add that would be a triple space.
i think i like double-space the best.
it dosen't
crowd
AND IT ISN'T

LOUD'!!!'!!!'.
I THINK it's the best.
causde it gives me a rest......
let's face it.
most people should double-space it.

This poem was the first one I typed on my Olivetti-Underwood typewriter in Lincoln Park, NJ. I named my new typewriter "Olive." (1968)

(1972)